For the Other 98%:

The Ultimate Guide for Student-Athletes to *Go Pro* in Entrepreneurship

Foreword by Kelvin Beachum Jr.

For the Other 98%: The Ultimate Guide for Student-Athletes to *Go Pro* in Entrepreneurship Copyright © 2017 by Krystal Beachum.

This book is a work of fiction. Names, characters, businesses, organiza- tions, places, events and incidents either are the product of the author's imagination or are used fictitiously. Any resemblance to actual persons, living or dead, events, or locales is entirely coincidental.

For information contact; www.studentathletesunite.com

ISBN: 978-1544913674

First Edition: February 2017

Table of Contents

Foreward

I am blessed to be part of the 2%. I am currently a five-year, NFL veteran playing for the New York Jets. I am a professional football player by occupation, but making a positive impact is my passion and my purpose. I attended Southern Methodist University in Dallas, Texas, where I received my Bachelors of Arts in Economics, and Masters in Liberal Studies. I spent my college years at SMU doubling as an involved student and dedicated athlete. Through my involvement as a student leader on the Student Athletic Advisory Committee, the SMU Board of Trustees, the President's Substance Abuse Task Force, Fellowship of Christian Athletes, and SMU Football team captain, I learned the art of juggling responsibilities. I also realized my vast and diverse areas of interest.

I am an agent for ending hunger, a youth mentor, a traveling speaker, and a minority youth advocate who supports Science, Technology,

Engineering, and Math (STEM) education, and career development. I have implemented advanced STEM curriculum and host annual STEM programs for my hometown school district, Mexia ISD, and for the Barack Obama Male Leadership Academy within Dallas ISD.

Welcome to this life-changing book. You are going to love it!

Being a student athlete is hard work. Being a professional athlete is rare. Becoming an entrepreneur is possible, and this book provides the blueprint. In these pages, you will learn to follow your passion, keep an open mind to new opportunities, fail fast and learn faster. You can immediately apply the life-changing principles and skills to your personal and professional life. It is helpful and easy to read, yet profound in its depth and clarity. Krystal approaches each chapter with a genuine heart, hope, direction, encouragement, and the necessary tools to go pro in entrepreneurship as a student-athlete.

I emphatically recommend "For the Other 98%", and plan to continue learning from the principles and direction outlined within. I pray that, as you read, your mind expands to make the most out of your life and the lives of those around you. Don't compromise what's cool, what's fun, or what's trending for what matters. Always focus on progress. Run your best race because there are no shortcuts. Be grateful because time is precious. Be responsible and leave a legacy. Be passionate because moderation is for cowards. Be innovative and change the game for the better. Be fearless because there is only one God. And lastly, practice patience and discipline. You enter college labeled as a student-athlete.

Create your own destiny to leave as an entrepreneur and business professional.

Kelvin Beachum
Servant Leader

Dedication

This book is dedicated to the student-athlete who is the dreamer, risk taker, believer and doer. The individual who is willing to work hard, overcome adversity and expects to make great things happen. May my words and advice empower you to live in your purpose and help you fulfill your dreams one lifetime at a time.

Introduction

Originally, I had not planned on writing this book until 2020. I knew I would be more successful than I already am, and it would make for a better book and story. I remember talking to one of my mentors and discussing my desire to write a book within the next five years. He said, "Why not now? People need to hear your wisdom now." I began to think how selfish it would be to wait until then in order for me to become more successful, rather than writing a book now that can impact thousands of athletes currently.

Sometimes we get so caught up in ourselves and the perfect time to do things, but I realized there isn't a perfect time. After many discussions, I decided to make this book more about you. I want to share my story with you, while also giving you the blueprint to create your own story by becoming the student-athlete entrepreneur. I have played basketball since the age of 9, and have created traits within playing that have helped mold me to who I am today. I have interviewed hundreds of former athletes who wish they had an option to learn about turning their passion into a business while also competing athletically.

Will do my best to provide you with the framework:

- Realize your gift
- Leverage your current resources
- Create your business

What are your next steps after reading this book?

If you are ready to become a student-athlete entrepreneur, then just go do it. However, I know that everyone is not meant to become an entrepreneur and that is okay. These chapters will still be beneficial in your life as a student-athlete, whether starting a business or not.

CHAPTER 1

The Employer OR The Employee

Entrepreneurs embody the promise of America; the belief that if you have a good idea and are willing to work hard and see it through, you can succeed in this country. And in fulfilling this promise, entrepreneurs also play a critical role in expanding our economy and creating jobs. – President Barack Obama

I grew up in a household that reflected two sides of the working world — an entrepreneur and an employee. My father has owned a mechanic business for more than 20 years now. Even with an 8th grade education, he has become one of the most successful black businessmen in our community. My father also referees high school, college basketball games part-time as a hobby, which pays pretty well might I add. My mother has been an employee of the state of Texas for more than 20 years, and she has her Associate and Bachelor's degree in Psychology.

Growing up, I saw the pros and cons of both careers. My mother was salary based while my father was performance based. My mother had holidays and weekends off, whereas my father rarely took off. As an entrepreneur, some weeks he did not get paid. However, that is usually the life of an entrepreneur. My mother's check would keep us afloat during these times. My siblings and I worked as employees of my father's business every school holiday, break and summers. We all saw his work ethic and his willingness to provide for his family.

Throughout his business career, he primarily handled business by himself. I saw my dad struggle, and the hard work he would put in as an entrepreneur still was not enough at times. I would remember thinking to myself why would anyone want to become an entrepreneur. I would rather work for someone else, because I know I am getting paid rather it be every week, two weeks or once a month. I remember every winter would be the hardest for my dad. There were weeks he didn't get paid and he would pick up extra games to help cover the cost. In the summer, business was always booming. I am assuming because everyone's cars would need their air conditioning fixed or their car would run hot due to the Texas heat.

Once I got to college, my mind started to shift. John D. Rockefeller once said, "I would rather earn 1 percent off 100 people's effort than 100 percent of my own efforts." I remember reading that quote while surfing the Internet to pass some time while in study hall during one of our away games for the Henderson State Women's basketball team. I realized then to become a wealthy entrepreneur, you need to build a team, concept or product/service that can function without you ever being there. My mind began to expand to ways I could possibly make that happen over the next few years.

A week after my 22nd birthday, I decided to start my first business. I started my first franchise for the price of dinner bill. My vacation pictures were my only inventory, natural hair was my overhead, my employees paid themselves, and my Instagram page was my business card. I created an income residually, while also growing my business across the states and internationally. When I was a kid, I wanted to be an adult. But, then I became an adult and lost freedom to jobs, bills, the need to impress others, dressing a certain way, and the list goes on. But then, I shifted my focus in life so I could feel like a kid again. Now I still have playtime. The classes are smaller, but the toys are bigger and my classmates and I have fun in different parts of the world.

Listen, there are so many blogs, articles and posts about how student-athletes are arguably the best candidates for any job. For most cases, it is true due to many of the characteristics athletes possess. However, I think society underestimates what we can truly provide to this world. The same skill set with the unique experiences that can make you a successful employee, can make you a successful entrepreneur.

Work Ethic

Depending if we were in pre-season, during season or off-season, my typical day as a Division II basketball player was 6 a.m. to 11 p.m. Those days were usually filled with early morning practice or weights, classes, film before practice, two-hour hour practices, film breakdown after practice, mandatory study hall, evening classes, and studying or finishing up homework for the next day. Then we'd go to sleep, and do the same routine over again. This was my life. That level of commitment is unmatched for any non-student-athlete. On LinkedIn, Andre Iguodala wrote the article "Athletes are built for more than sports. Here's why we need to become businessmen, too." In it, he states, "Our work ethic is unparalleled, and we are gifted with an exceptional degree of aspiration and drive, suited for any profession."

Adaptability

Sports teaches you to prepare for the unexpected, adjust quickly and be flexible. At Henderson, I went through three coaches in three years. That was truly a learning experience for a few of my teammates and me. Adaptability also comes in handy when you are playing your sport.

You think a team is going to play a certain defense or go through with certain plays, but then you realize they have come up with all types of stuff that you and your team didn't go over in practice. Yes, the scouting reports you had for the other team did not really help much at all this time. After the first half time, you make half-time adjustments to become more effective in the next half. Being able to adapt and make the best of the situation while staying committed to what you do/know best is crucial for an employee whether working as an intern, a CEO or as an entrepreneur starting his or her own business.

Understanding Failure

My father always taught us, "You have to learn how to lose, before you learn how to win." I really think he used to tell us that to make us feel better about losing, and to keep us humble whenever we did win big games. Personal growth comes from learning from your mistakes. Everyone loses in his or her life, but what you learn from it determines your future. You only fail when you stop trying. In fact, Richard Branson (founder of the Virgin Group) made a great analogy when referring to the game of tennis to business. He said, "One key lesson I've learned, which applies far beyond the court, is to treat each point separately. Forget the last mistake and move onto the next challenge. Tennis, like business, moves so quickly that if you dwell on the past for even a few minutes, an opportunity will have passed and the moment will be lost."

Coachable

The high school athlete will get to college on pure will and God given talent, but it will take a lot more for the athlete to stay in the athletic program. As an athlete, we have to take constructive criticism from our coaches and apply them to our game. If that doesn't happen, then you probably will not play or you may just get dropped from the team. This applies to entrepreneurship as well. You have to be able to take feedback from your customers, and take advice from your team and mentors to help grow your business.

Mental Toughness

This term cannot be easily taught. Mental toughness is used when competing within our minds, against teammates and opposing teams. This is the spirit that instills durability, endurance and overcoming adversity in the student-athlete. For example, I remember tearing my ACL, MCL, inner and outer meniscus, and cartilage my senior year of high school. I can remember the frustration, pain and the uncertainty to ever be able to play at the level I was accustomed to playing. It took me over a year to recover, but I came back better than before with stats to prove it. Coming back from any injury that continues to play at a high level exemplifies the true meaning of mental toughness. Richard Branson notes, "Treat business like sport – follow your passions, keep an open mind to new opportunities, and refuse to take no for an answer."

Teamwork

If you were to describe the team you would like to be a part of, what type of team would it be? A football or baseball team that is highly dependent on each other, or a track team where individual performances adds up to team efforts? There is no right or wrong answer because as teammates, we all depend on each other to win in our sport. With the shift toward owning a business, collaboration with your team or employees plays a big part in the expansion of your business.

Teamwork also goes hand-in-hand with your support system, like your family, friends and significant other. Without them, most student-athletes cannot become successful. All my mentors who are successful entrepreneurs also have a support system that work together as a team. As a family, they come up with a game plan to do business, while also allotting enough time to spend time with their family.

Goal Setter

I never really got to play basketball for fun. I always spent countless hours learning to improve how I played the game. As an individual and a team, we set daily, weekly, monthly and yearly goals. It didn't matter how big or small the goals were, they were measurable and attainable. As athletes, we usually keep our goals close by to check and to follow up to see if we are close to accomplishing them or have already. By doing this, it holds us accountable for what we have done or not done. Even two years removed from college athletics, I still make goals. It is usually in the form of a to-do list, short-term and long-term goals, and a five-year plan.

To be honest, I may be biased about student-athletes being entrepreneurs over employees. According to the NCAA, more than 480,000 compete as NCAA athletes, and just a select few within each sport move on to compete at the professional or Olympic level. Take a look at the chart below:

Estimated Probability of Competing in Professional Athletics

	NCAA Participants	Approximate # Draft Eligible	# Draft Picks	# NCAA Drafted	% NCAA to Major Pro*	% NCAA to Total Pro^
Football	72,788	16,175	256	256	1.6%	1.9%
M Basketball	18,697	4,155	60	46	1.1%	12.2%
W Basketball	16,589	3,686	36	33	0.9%	4.7%
Baseball	34,198	7,600	1,215	738	9.7%	--
M Ice Hockey	4,071	905	210	60	6.6%	--
M Soccer	24,477	5,439	75	75	1.4%	--

Percent NCAA to Major Pro figures are based on the number of draft picks made in the NFL, NBA, WNBA, MLB, NHL and MLS drafts only.

After reading the Huffington Post article "What If Entrepreneurship Can Be Used to Help NCAA Athletes Achieve More?," these questions still remain: What happens with the other 90-99 percent of college athletes after their eligibility is up? What is being done to make sure their talents are being utilized beyond the playing field? Once the athlete's eligibility is up, most graduate from college or is offered a post-graduate scholarship to finish his or her degree. Once finished, they go on to participate in different pro leagues or get a job. If you sleep eight hours a day and work a job you do not care for much for eight hours a day, then out of one year, that takes up approximately eight months. Do the math. My hope for any athlete after reading this book will be for you to understand that you playing small does not serve the world. The world needs your innovation, creativity and revolutionary ideas. Being an entrepreneur is hard, but so is being a collegiate athlete. If you can use the same skills you've developed while playing sports, there is no doubt in my mind that you can become a successful entrepreneur.

CHAPTER 2

Network Equals Your Net Worth

"God has already lined up all the people in your path to get you to your dreams and vision; all you have to do is get rid of the wrong ones."

–Steve Harvey

AT the age of 22, I had a couple of mentors who taught me things about what most people would call "the real world," and how it really works. People think of networking and saying you have a number or a contact, but it's so much more than that. I was told it is not about who you know, but who knows you. My first lesson was: Leaders are Readers. One of the first books I was told to read when thinking of starting a business was "Rich Dad, Poor Dad" by Robert Kiyosaki. That is the first book I read on financial education and I highly recommend you read it as well.

In summary, the books talks about what the rich teach their children about money and what the poor and middle class do not. I guess you thought I was going to give you the whole synopsis of the book so you would not have to go read it yourself. Well, then you would not learn anything. Right? But one of his quotes that really stood out to me was "The richest people in the world build networks; everyone else is trained to look for work." That quote changed my mindset and way of thinking.

I really wish I read this sooner. Please do not misunderstand the quote. All he is saying is that Oprah, Richard Branson, Donald Trump, Russell Simmons, Bill Gates, Mark Zuckerberg, and many more wealthy people were blessed to network and find people who were smarter than they were and helped them to execute the vision that have. Always remember, the bigger the network, the bigger your NET WORTH.

I am about to tell you three effective ways to help build your network on any college campus as an athlete. I cannot make this stuff up. But first, you have to serve others without looking for something in return. You can only succeed in these three steps when you put others' needs before your own.

Athletic Involvement

Regardless if an athlete is playing Division I, Division II, Division III, NAIA, or at a junior college, every school has an athletic director and compliance officer. GO MEET THEM or email them if they are not in their office. You just start with an introduction of yourself, where you are from, and what you hope to accomplish while attending that college or university. Then end with asking, "Is there anything I can help you with?" People love getting help when they don't have to pay for it or come out of budget. Believe me. Building a relationship with any of the staff or administrators would be a great start to being involved. Most schools have Fellowship of Christian Athletes (FCA) and Student-Athlete Advisory Committee (SAAC). I've built relationships and friendships through these two organizations that have helped launch and grow my businesses.

Athletes have so many resources available, and sometimes, they take them for granted. Usually institutions of higher education host workshops and bring in speakers to help the student-athletes. Take advantage of that. Go introduce yourself to that keynote speaker; take business cards from people at the workshops. Always be strategic in networking and building relationships. I remember after every home game, I would go thank all of the athletic staff, administrators and coaches of other sports for coming to our game. I realized they did not have to show support, but they did. Even if I did not get a chance to speak to them and thank them, I would go by the office next day or send an email thanking them for their time. A lot of little things usually go a long way.

WRITE DOWN THREE THINGS YOU WILL DO TO BECOME INVOLVED THROUGH ATHLETICS?

1. _____

2. _____

3. _____

Community Involvement

Colleges and universities love to showcase their athletes giving back to the community, participating in food drives and helping those less fortunate. As a former athlete, I felt like I was made to do a lot of those things. Do not get me wrong, I enjoyed the feeling afterward, but nobody likes to be told what to do. However, you can take a different approach. Go online and look up volunteer opportunities in the area. You are taking the initiative to research volunteering yourself, and looking for opportunities that interest you. Plus, it is always a great resume builder.

You should always pick somewhere you can see yourself volunteering for a long period of time, which is usually three-six months. Each school year is around nine months, so you may go home for the summer. If you could volunteer for an hour a month, or every six weeks, I am sure that organization would be appreciative. You will not only build a relationship with the staff, but also build trust. In the end, you may actually use someone at that organization for a reference.

Depending on where you are going to school, there are usually networking events, and FREE functions going on around town. Of course, you can either go online or find them in the local/school newspaper. As an athlete, you are usually not from the area. Networking and building relationships with the local residents can show you all the good food places to dine, places to get your hair done or cut, good churches and introduce you to other local residents. Make sure you surround yourself with like-minded people as well. They will keep you sane when you had a bad game, trouble with your coach, or if you need someone to speak with. They really serve as an outlet to our journey through college athletics.

WRITE DOWN THREE THINGS YOU WILL DO TO BECOME INVOLVED THROUGH YOUR COMMUNITY?

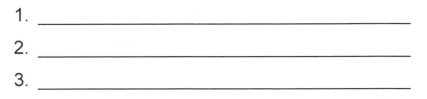

1. _____

2. _____

3. _____

Campus Involvement

This will sound cliché, but I guess you can say I saved the best for last. Let's face it, depending on which sport you play, you will be recognized around campus. Sometimes, student-athletes are seen as athletes and nothing more. I think the time is now to change the narrative. Go meet your professors. And no, I am not talking about the handshake you give them on the first day of class and say, "Hi, my name is Krystal Beachum and I play for the basketball team here." I am talking about actually going to their office during office hours, sitting down and having a conversation with them. Show them your athletic schedule, talk about the syllabus, let them know you are going to work in their class and what you expect to get out of this class. I promise, not only will this help you throughout the season, but you can also build that relationship to where you can possibly ask for a letter of recommendation.

I had a couple teammates and other former athletes I have interviewed over the last year that said there are not enough resources to help athletes. However, there are so many organizations and clubs on campuses that encompass every hobby or passion possible. It is so easy to access the information. You can type into Google search "student organizations at [name of college/university]" and a link will come up every time. Most have emails to either the student president or faculty advisor email. Most organizations or clubs can be joined at no cost, and meet once a month or every two weeks. It may be hard to make it when you are in season, but it should be no reason to join a club or organization once off-season comes around.

Before I even stepped foot on Henderson State University's campus, I did this exact same thing. I went through the list and highlighted all of the organizations or clubs that I was interested in. I either emailed the president or I looked out for the next meeting on the flyer that was hanging up on the information wall. Every student-athlete has the access and the resources. Will you go out and grow your network while in college?

Maintaining Your Network

Anyone can meet someone and have a conversation with him or her, but the hardest thing to do is actually maintaining and cultivating the relationship. I am just going to let you all in on a little secret I do when I first meet people. Before I begin, if you haven't read "How to Win and Influence Friends" by Dale Carnegie then that should be on your book list as well. One thing I learned from this book is to become genuinely interested in other people and be a good listener. Mr. Carnegie wrote, "You can make more friends in two months by being interested in them, than in two years by making them interested in you."

I really dislike those people at conferences, workshops or networking events who go around and try to meet everyone in less than an hour to scurry up business cards. Those are the people you need to stay away from because they are not personable. If you actually want to start and maintain your relationships, then always focus on three-five people that look interesting to you and you get to know them. I usually start by asking, "How are you doing today?"

Then I follow with a series of questions:

"What do you do? Where do you work?"

"How do you like your job? How long have you worked there?"

"Are you from this area?"

If so, I ask, "How long you've lived here?" If not, I ask, "how long has it been since you've moved to the area?"

"What do you do for fun?"

Depending on what they do for fun, I would say, "That's great! Me too! We should go grab lunch or coffee together." We usually exchange contact information. After meeting a person, I write down everything we talked about or that I remember about him or her in my note section of his or her contact information. I then email/call/text him or her within the first 24-48 hours of our first encounter. I always put the place we meet, then mention something that would trigger his or her memory when reading your email.

For example:

Good morning Ms. Angela,

It was a pleasure meeting you and learning more about what you do for college students. The transition program is much needed. I was hoping to get your contact information during the Saturday night event, but I guess I stayed on the dance floor too long!

I did find your email on the pamphlet that you gave me. I will definitely be spreading the word about the program to people who I know are struggling to find work. Thank you again for all that you do. Talk soon.

Best Wishes,
Krystal Beachum

After the first encounter, you really don't know that person too well. Invite him or her to coffee, brunch or lunch. Everyone LOVES free food. You want him or her to be a part of your network. If you can, always pay for the food. I know what you are thinking! Most athletes are either living from Pell

Grant to Pell Grant or monthly stipend to monthly stipend. Some may even be living from loan check to loan check. Trust me on this, I know your struggle, but buying an extra $5 coffee will not kill your pocketbook. What has made me so successful in building a network is that I give more than I take. I will give my time, resources and money. Anyone that knows me can attest to that.

Once you start to develop those relationships, begin to follow through on everything. Let's not forget the lost art of writing personalized thank you notes. That goes a long way with every aspect of networking and can make you memorable. I met a girl that once told me that she tracks all of her conversations with people. She reaches out to her contacts every six weeks just to follow up, as well as keeping up with what they are doing with their lives. I know this seems like a lot of work. I am sure if you ever think about starting a business or choosing a career, then you will thank me later.

Keep in mind, you may not need to reach out to 200 people every six weeks, but choose eight to ten relationships you want to make strong and cultivate those. My mentor once told me to only talk to the ones often that will take you to the next level. My eight to ten strong relationships have now developed into my mentors. I think that is the most rewarding part of network building. You will soon figure it out for yourself.

CHAPTER 3

From Branding to Business

"Creating content that allows us to share our experiences, thoughts, and ideas in real time is becoming an intrinsic part of life in the 21st century. – Gary Vaynerchuk

Social media is a big part of everyone's life, especially of a student-athlete's career. However, many athletes are just told by their team, "Be careful what you put out there. We're watching you!" The problem is that athletes are not told how to post items that are professional in appearance. This chapter can specifically teach athletes how to use social media to professionally brand themselves while promoting their business.

Before getting into ways to build your brand or promoting your business, as an athlete you have to understand the power of influence you already have. Whether you are at a NAIA school or at a big

Division I school, you have a platform. The athletic department loves you, your peers and professors respect you, and the community loves you like a college running back— as Drake would say. Every athlete has at least one account on a social media networking site such as Facebook, Instagram, Twitter, Snapchat, Tumblr, etc. Here are some examples of what you should be posting online and if anything doesn't fit in line with what I have written below, then it should not be posted on social media:

1. Say thank you.

This is always a good option. Student-athletes should take time to thank those who support them. Fans, teammates and family for example.

2. Support others.

Student-athletes can provide a positive example for other students by sending positive messages about their peers in other sports or activities at school.

3. Share news and humor.

Social media is meant to be fun. Join in

conversations and share things you find interesting or entertaining.

4. Engage in discussion with those you admire.

It was difficult to interact or even hear from famous people that student-athletes admire. But now, they can follow them on Twitter and learn what they're discussing and even interact with them.

5. Post anything consistent with your personal brand.

Again, how do you want to present yourself in public? You want people to gather a sense of who you are and what you do based on your social media. If you are an athlete, but aspiring to be a health trainer. Then you need to make post about you playing your sport, training in the gym, facts about eating healthy and training people. Your timeline should be filled with posts like those, and with the other four things I just shared about what needs to be posted on social media.

As you are building your brand on social media, you need to think about what makes you different from all other athletes. It's important to take a proactive role and to continue to build it in a way that best supports your athletic career. You want people to talk about you as much as possible, but in a positive way. To help you get started, answer these questions. Then make sure all your social media posts show the real you!

- What are my top values?
- What adjectives do people consistently use when describing you?
- What is my main goal to achieve on social media to build my brand?

Your years on social media can either cost you money or make you money. For example, actively managing your social media increases the numbers of fans and followers you have and in turn, make you more popular and sought out for certain opportunities. However, if used in a negative manner, then it will cause fans and followers to repel and not follow you. In turn, damage your brand and business if you choose to create one. We live in an age that everything is at our fingertips with our phones. Social media is creating wealth, fame and celebrity status for a lot of people around the globe. Social media is allowing young people to create opportunities for themselves.

Signing on to be a college athlete automatically projects you into the spotlight. You have the Booster Club members, alumni, athletic staff, parents, kids and college students following your every move on social media. But, how can you reach a broader audience through your social media following? I'm about to let you in on a little secret of what I have been implementing within my social media, especially Instagram thanks to David Shands (founder of Sleep is for Suckers). I will tell you more about him in the later chapter.

Facebook

You should have your Facebook page linked to your Instagram page. Why? Because your followers on Facebook and your followers on Instagram aren't the same people. Once you link those two, your friends on Facebook will see it. They may see it and have an Instagram as well and follow you.

Hashtags:

Start using hastags on Instagram and Twitter. On Instagram, you can use up to 30 hashtags per picture. If you do not want to put them under your initial caption, then you can put them in the comment section. So if you decided to be a part of the travel industry, you should hashtag travel, beaches, oceans, wanderlust, vacation, cruises. People who are looking at travel hashtags may stumble across what you do. If you ever decide to look at a few of my posts, you will see that I use hashtags on all of my photos. I also use hashtags for different posts whether it is travel, family, sports, networking or speaking engagements.

Engagement

As athletes, we have this bad. If someone comments on your post, comment back. I know some of you may get those weird comments from those kids saying, "I am your biggest fan. It would make my day if you could respond." A simple "hello" would be nice. It is just polite and the nice thing to do. Here's a perfect analogy: When you are walking and you make eye contact with that person, in turn you say, "hello." Then they just give you that awkward smile and do not say "hello" back. Or you open a door for someone and they do not say "thank you." Let's not be one of those people on social media. We get busy throughout the day, but it does not take long to reply back depending on how many comments you have. Unless it is an emoji, because that is tricky, I am still trying to figure out if I need to send one back or not even comment.

While I am also on engagement, I need for you to "like" other people's post. I was that person who would only get on social media to post a photo and get right back off. Now, I just go down my timeline and "like" everyone's post. Most of the time I do not even like the post or sometimes that person. Sometimes, I do not even look at what people post anymore, I just start to "like" away. The reason for that is because they are on Instagram if they just posted, and when you "like" their post, then they also know you are on Instagram. In exchange, they may work their way over to your page and "like" your pictures. It will then drive your "likes" up and they will start thinking you are both on the same page because of the "like exchange."

Timing

The time of day is very important to get the most interaction from your social media pages. There are different times of the day when I post on all my social media accounts. For example, I know 6-9 p.m. is the best time for me to post on Facebook. People are usually off work, and they are relaxing before going to bed for the next day by 9 p.m. The best time for Saturday is around 9 a.m. because everyone is still lying in bed. Around 1 p.m. on Sundays are the best because most of my Facebook friends should be out of church and eating around this time. I have been using this schedule for more than a year now and the engagement is great.

You can research the best times to post on social media and a calendar with all the times for each outlet will come up. Actually, go to Google right now and type in the "best time to post on social media." You can use that as your tester and once you start seeing the pattern, then you can make adjustments. There is also an app that I recently started using called "When to Post." It tells you the best time of engagement on your timeline. How cool is that?

Candid Shots (also known as) Off guard photos

Don't act like you don't take those off guard photos where you are looking at your watch or looking down at the ground. We all do it, no worries. People always want to take a look behind the scenes of the athlete's life. They want to feel like they are a part of your life and your family too. So take those photos when you are with the family, speaking to little children, having an intense dance off with your teammates. Then add a dope caption, and there goes your "likes". You are giving them the backstage pass into your life. Don't be afraid of social media. It is free marketing, not only for your brand as a student-athlete, but even if you are thinking about becoming an entrepreneur. Start implementing these strategies into your social media. I promise you will not regret it.

I remember when I first started my business and I attempted to use social media to grow it as well. You see I used the word "attempt" because it was an epic fail. Through my social media, I was saying, "Buy my product; you need my product. If you do not buy my product or what I am selling, then you are going to die." I am totally kidding, I never said that, but I was getting on my follower's nerves because I was trying to sell them through social media. I quickly learned that it is called SOCIAL media, NOT "selling" media. Believe me, there are pages that I come across now that make me cringe and show you what NOT to do.

I began studying the power of social media and the people that were experts in building their business through social media. I then came across Gary Vaynerchuk, he is the GURU of social media marketing. On top of that, he is an investor and best-selling author. His book, "Jab, Jab, Jab, Right Hook: How to Tell Your Story in a Noisy Social World," has changed my life. Every social media platform is different, and he teaches you exactly how to expand your business on each platform. A disclaimer: I know for a fact that I am not the best marketer in the world, but I am so much better than what I was four years ago, and I have been studying and learning from the best. There are many ways to grow your business through social media, but I have narrowed them down to the top three and most important.

1. Provide value and content to your audience

Our society has a selfish generation where it seems like everything revolves around only us, hence the word "selfie." Regardless if you are building a brand, working with a company or becoming an entrepreneur, we have to become self-less. If all you do is build a page or profile to sell, market or promote, you will not have very much of a following and you will not build your business. In the words of the late Zig Ziglar, "You will get all you want in life if you help enough other people get what they want."

2. Tailored content on each social media platform.

It is important to understand that every social media platform is unique and requires a unique formula. "What works on Facebook won't necessarily work on Twitter," explains Vaynerchuk. Similarly, stories told through pictures on Instagram do not resonate the same way when told in an identical manner on Pinterest. To someone who is not familiar to the social media world, they would assume that all social media platforms are alike, and in many ways they are. Almost every social media platform has some type of photo-sharing, but each one cultivates a unique sensibility and style. Some sites allow hyperlinks, while others don't.

"Content is king, but context is God," writes Gary. "You can put out good content, but if it ignores the context of the platform on which it appears, it can easily fall flat."

Here are the content/social network pairings Vaynerchuk suggested:

- Animated gifs on Tumblr
- Infographics on Pinterest
- Great photos and quote cards on Instagram
- Everything works on Facebook
- Quotes and really smart hashtag usage on Twitter

3. Use Social Media as "Social Proof"

I believe this is the most important step you can use to grow your business through social media. Social media is supposed to be branding yourself and your business while being you and having fun. You can create social proof by posting all the benefits you are getting from your business or product. Essentially, live your lifestyle and live vicariously through yourself, but at the same time, build your brand by including some things that have something to do with your business periodically. Positivity and living in your purpose is contagious, and people will definitely follow you for those same reasons.

If you feel like you do not have the lifestyle or the results you want to share on your page currently, you have two options: You can post information about the path you are on and the goals you are working toward, which works in a similar way to posting the actual results. You can mention people who do have the results you are trying to achieve from time to time, so that people can see those you are surrounding yourself with. Do not let the lack of experience or lack of results deter you from creating your brand or promoting your business.

There are so many examples I can use when trying to explain to an athlete about how you can make your social media benefit your social network. Maybe I should just use my own experience. I started following this Instagram page called Messages from Beezy roughly three years ago while I was still playing basketball at Henderson State. The Messages from Breezy is a motivational movement inspiring one wristband at a time. I love supporting entrepreneurs, even if I do not know them. I purchased a couple bands for myself, and a few for my teammates. To this day, I have never met Mike Hairston, the CEO of The Messages from Breezy in person, but I have seen his brand and social media presence grow. He continues to inspire thousands of people with his message. I am sure his story will motivate you as well.

I reached out to him through social media to ask him about his story and told him that his story needs to be told and would like to feature him in my book. He agreed and began telling me, "I would have never imagined that I would be graduating from the University of Arkansas four years ago. I was a lost soul who just loved playing basketball, baseball and making people laugh. As bad as I wanted to continue my collegiate athletic career, God had a better plan for me. The reason why I started my business was because I had a passion for motivating and inspiring the ones who were close to me, my friends, my family and my teammates. I thought that since the verse, 'All things are possible, if you believe (Mark 9:23),' resonated with me, I knew it would have an impact on other people's lives as well. Messages From Beezy/The Beezy Brand began with just a blog on July 24, 2013, and shortly after, wristbands began selling all across the world.

"I first started with the close contacts that I have around me, like friends and family, and later began pursuing well-rounded athletes and individuals at the University of Arkansas. I have used social media to expand the business by promoting individual's testimonies, products and current events happening around the world. I like to keep things current and tie everyone together. I realized that time management is so crucial when starting on the road to entrepreneurship. Over the years, I have accounted the fact that I am different than other people my age. Not everyone begins a business and movement, so managing my time has become very important. What I have earned from my experience so far is that I am an advocate for communicating and listening to others. I find much joy and excitement of listening to where people have come from and the journey they took to get to where they are now. I am very honored that so many have felt comfortable enough to open up and tell me how they have believed in the band. I recommend a student-athlete who is pursuing entrepreneurship to manage their time and stay faithful to God. There will be many days where you feel like giving up and taking the easy way out, but you can't. When you factor in how many people are motivated and inspired by what you are doing, you can not give up on them. Most importantly, you can not give up on God and the plan that He has for your life. Lastly, I would like to truly say "All things are possible, to Him who believes." The people that He has placed in my life have truly humbled my walk and I am grateful for all of the things He has done for me. Never give up and always give glory to God. Upon graduation, I will continue to expand my brand and entrepreneurship.

Reaching out to Mike Hairston and getting his incredible story all evolved from a simple follow and support from three years ago. Always remember to use social media for what is built for, which is to create a network and build genuine relationships."

CHAPTER 4

Connecting Passion to Your Purpose

-*"If you don't love what you do, you won't do it with much conviction or passion."* –Mia Hamm

People tell us to do what we love and follow our passion. No matter if you are aspiring to be an entrepreneur or just becoming the best version of yourself, you will need to know your passion and your purpose. You know the old saying, "Follow your passion, and the money will come?" This is true. However, if there is no purpose behind any of your passions, you will not be happy or successful. Following your passion while living out your purpose is the ultimate goal. During my time as an academic counselor, I had a few athletes struggling to find their passion and purpose and wondered what they were going to do after their college athletic career was complete. I took them into an empty room and brought a blank sheet of paper with me. I closed the door and asked them, "If money didn't exist, what would you for the rest of your life?"

I must admit, you should have seen the look on some of their faces. They told me to repeat the question. I guess they wanted to make sure they heard it right the first time. I asked again, "If money didn't exist, what would you do for the rest of your life?" Some of the answers were interesting. One of the girls loved dolphins and wanted to be a dolphin trainer. Another one said she was good at creeping and finding out information on anyone and wanted to become an FBI agent. I had a few that wanted to play their sport for the rest of their life. Unfortunantly, being able to play a sport for the rest of your life, is nearly impossible due to the fact that your body just will not be able to. Kobe Byrant, Michael Phelps, Abby Wambach, and Tamika Catchings retired within the last year, so regardless of sport, your time may come to retire and move on to other passions.

Anyone can identify passion by these three things: Childhood dreams, knowing the difference between a hobby and profitable passion, and if you like teaching others about your passion.

Childhood Dreams

Growing up, I wanted to be and create so many things. I wanted to be a WNBA player, an author, work with the FBI, and be a middle or high school history teacher; I wanted to travel the world and create a nonprofit to give back to the community. As I am writing this, I am wondering when would I have time to become all of these things in one lifetime. However, those were my childhood dreams. Usually, when we grow up, reality sets in, and we forget about what we once dreamed of as a child. To identify your passion, close your eyes and try to remember what are some things you wanted to do or wanted to create as a child. Write those down. That will help you in the next step.

Hobbies and Profitable Passions

My mentor once told me that hobbies cost money. So you have to know the difference between a hobby and a profitable passion. I am not going to lie; I wrote "to nap" as one of my hobbies in college. Every athlete knows a nap throughout the day can make a difference in how you practice and if you will have enough energy to do homework that night. I am sure you have hobbies that you do that will never benefit you in the future. Make sure you are aware. For example, my hobbies used to be napping and binge-watching Law & Order: SVU and Criminal Minds. I would spend hours watching episodes, even though I would have seen some of them multiple times. During all those hours spent watching television, I could have used to grow my profitable passion. Now, write down a few of your passions that could possibly make you a profit.

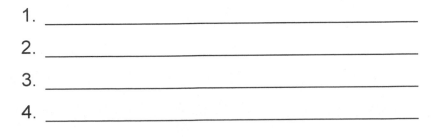

1. _____

2. _____

3. _____

4. _____

5. _____

Teach Others About Your Passion

There is a Chinese proverb that says, "Give a man a fish and you feed him for a day. Teach a man to fish, and you feed him for a lifetime." In today's world, everything can be self-taught. In actuality, you do not have to college to learn a lot of things. Everything is accessible through the Internet or your local library. All you need to get is a library card. However, since athletes use college to earn a degree and to possibly go to the next level, then I will explain ways how to use college to benefit you the most in a later chapter. Everyone wants to become better, whether it is a better writer, athlete, spouse, teacher — whatever you can think of. There is always room for experts in your particular area of passion. If you cannot help but talk and want to teach everyone about what you are learning, then that is also one of your passions.

Passion is what you are doing, and purpose is the reason you are doing it. Since you have already written down some things you are passion about, let's discover your purpose. In finding your purpose, you must become reflective. Take some time for yourself and find a place that you can be most reflective. Being reflective is asking these questions: "Why am I on this earth? What are some things that I can do to change the world? What is my greatest value?" Without purpose, your passion will not work. We are all equipped with gifts, talents and unbelievable potential. It is up to you to find yours.

A good friend of mine sent me a video of Steve Harvey talking to a college student. Steve told the young man, "What burns in your heart is important for you to pay attention to because it never goes away." Since college is a period of discovery, he suggested to all college students to spend a lot of time discovering their respective gifts. If you wake up pursuing your math, you are going to have a rough life. That is why people wake up in a rut and their lives may have no purpose or meaning. Steve added that some people are not "morning persons" because they are not living in their purpose. People are waking up and do not know the reason or have any design in mind. Once you live in your purpose, you ca not wait to wake up; or when you do wake up, you are happy about waking up. The comedian also suggests paying close attention to what makes you happy and pursuing your degree. "But also take a look on what burns on the inside of you," he concludes. "Do not ignore the things that burn within you and pursue it with everything in you."

Finding your passion and purpose are both equally important to becoming a successful student-athlete entrepreneur or just improving the overall quality of your life. As we grow older, society puts us in a box. Society tells us we are suppose to go to school, get good grades, get a good job, work 40-50 years for a company, retire and then live off of 40 percent of our salary until we die. Our parents do it, our grandparents also did it, and most likely our great grandparents did it as well. Over the last few years, I have found that most of the people I wanted to become either had a lot of money and no time or a lot of time and no money. I also found out that there were so many former student-athletes who were unhappy with their current lives. Not only have they not fulfilled their purpose, but they did not follow their passion. Now they are unsatisfied with their current situation because they went along with what society wanted for them.

Growing up, I had always planned to be a middle school history teacher. Even though I loved the game of basketball, I did not want to become a basketball coach. Imagine that. I remember I would put all my teddy bears and dolls in rows and put pen and paper in front of them. I would imagine I was in front of the classroom teaching about the infamous Civil War and the great generals of that era. I had envisioned myself helping my young children create projects, and watch them grow from the beginning of the school year until the last day of class. I even had the perfect method of handling children who did noy obey. I would just send them to the principal's office or put them in time out. Little did I know, sometimes that does not even help the child at all. Every time someone would ask me what I wanted to be, I would say, "A middle school teacher." My family supported that decision. They felt like I would be perfect for the job because of my creativity and because I was very patient.

When I was getting recruited in high school, the passion for teaching children did not change. Thankfully, every school I was looking into had an education program. After my injury, I decided to go to junior college and was able to get my basic core classes out the way. The beginning of my second year, I was preparing to get recruited again to a four-year institution. Because I red shirted my first year at my junior college, I was able to have three years at the next university. After much thought, I decided to attend Henderson State University, a Division II school in Arkansas, rather than a Division I school in Virginia. It was closer to home, and the Teachers College was one of the best in Arkansas. I moved there in hopes of finally pursing my purpose and being able to make an impact of the future generation of children.

I enrolled in the Middle Level Education: Social Studies and Language Arts program. At the top of my transcript, it had bachelor's of education will be completed by May 2014. At first, I was not too happy about all the credits I had to take in order to finally get that degree. However, I was excited because I knew that over time I could finally say I was a teacher. The classes were great, teachers were interactive and I learned a lot from all of our projects. Then, along came the Praxis. That exam cost me so much money. I am sure I spent well over $1,000 for testing. In order for you to become a teacher, you have to pass all three parts of the Praxis. For Part 1, there are three sections and I kept failing one of those three sections. Finally after the seventh time, I was finally able to pass it and start taking classes to bring me closer to my purpose.

During my junior year, I felt like my purpose began to change. I was doing everything I was told to do in order to be successful in life — or so I thought. I had a 3.8 GPA at the time, a starter for the basketball team, involved in multiple committees and honor societies, president of the Student-Athlete Advisory Committee (SAAC), and volunteering my time at local organizations. On the outside looking in, you would have thought Krystal knows what she wants in life. However, I felt empty and unsatisfied with my life. I knew I was destined for more and knew I could impact people on a global scale. I just did not know how it would come to life. I still wanted to impact children, but instead of asking them what they wanted to be when they grew up, I wanted to ask them, "What do you want to create when you grow up?" and help them to do that for themselves. I remember trying to switch majors and my counselor advising me that it would take more time if I switched majors. After talking it over with my mom, I told her I would finish with my Bachelors of Education and then possibly go into a Master's program in something else. When the second part of the Praxis reared its ugly head, I passed the first section with flying colors, but failed the second part. In order for me to take the next step into internship, I needed to pass both parts.

The time came for me to finally know my fate after taking the Praxis before going into my last semester of internship. I read the score, and all I remember was that it was not enough to pass. I was devastated because my parents did not raise a quitter. I remember walking to the car and calling my mom. She knew as soon as she heard my voice that I had failed. All I could do was cry. I went to go tell my head coach about what happened and broke down crying again. I had to go tell the Dean of the Teachers College I had failed and could not begin my internship. We talked about the different options that I could possibly do. I could either graduate in May with a General Studies degree or I could take some "blow-off classes" this semester, pass the Praxis 2 and participate in my internship in the fall.

I had to make the decision the same day because we had a road game and I would not be back until the following week. I decided to change my major to General Studies because I did not want to wait another semester to graduate. I had also planned to go to graduate school to pursue my Master's degree. At first, I felt ashamed and embarrassed because I was almost to the finish line and I couldn't even cross it. My parents have always supported my decisions. I remember my mom said, "Your heart was not fully into being a teacher anymore and I realized that. That is why God did not allow you to finish the journey at this time." I felt a little better because my mom knew how I felt.

Your passions and purpose may not tie into your degree at all, and that is okay. In the midst of all this chaos, I was also able to identify three of my passions. If you remember earlier in the chapter, I talked about my childhood dreams. I have always wanted to travel and help people along the way. I am also passionate about student-athletes and entrepreneurship. Let's just say that all three passions have been beneficial in my life and molded me to who I am now. The beginning of my entrepreneurial journey was rough.

As a student-athlete, along with being an entrepreneur, was one of the hardest challenges because everything is about your mentality. There were negative people and naysayers during that time, but I did not let that get in my way. There were a lot of people I considered family, spent time with and helped out, but they did not support my business. You should remember that nine times out 10, your friends will not be in your business target demographic. As I matured, I finally realized that nobody owed me anything. Looking back, I am thankful for the journey so far, and it has taught me that everyone will not see your vision; that is okay. I must admit that now I can see the future in my present. Because of where I came from, I understand that everything that happens to me today is for someone else to benefit from tomorrow.

If you do not have your passion or purpose, I encourage you to take some time to realize them. Once you have it, write it out in the space below.

CHAPTER 5

Asking the Right Questions

*"We must be student-centered in all that we do …
We have to collectively deliver on those promises.
That's what you care about. That's why we're in this
business" – President Mark Emmert, NCAA*

There are a lot of rules and regulations regarding the student-athlete entrepreneur and the NCAA. If done right way, which is by getting approval, an athlete can and will be able to own a business while playing collegiately. As athletes, we go to school, study and spend up to 30-60 hours a week on our sport. I know there is little time to get a job, so even talking about building a business is nearly impossible. However, it is definitely possible through time management, social media and your network. Below I have added the rules needed for each division of the NCAA to help you understand what you can and cannot do.

Division I

12.4.1 Criteria Governing Compensation to Student-Athletes. Compensation may be paid to a student-athlete: (Revised: 11/22/04)

1. (a) Only for work actually performed; and
2. (b) At a rate commensurate with the going rate in that locality for similar services.

12.4.1.1 Athletics Reputation. Such compensation may not include any remuneration for value or utility that the student-athlete may have for the employer because of the publicity, reputation, fame or personal follow- ing that he or she has obtained because of athletics ability.

12.4.2.1 Fee-for-Lesson Instruction. A student-athlete may receive compensation for teaching or coaching sports skills or techniques in his or her sport on a fee-for-lesson basis, provided: [R] (Revised: 1/9/96 effective 8/1/96, 4/25/02 effective

8/1/02, 4/2/03 effective 8/1/03)

1. (a) Institutional facilities are not used;

2. (b) Playing lessons shall not be permitted;

3. (c) The institution obtains and keeps on file documentation of the recipient of the lesson(s) and the fee for the lesson(s) provided during any time of the year;

4. (d) The compensation is paid by the lesson recipient (or the recipient's family) and not another individual or entity;

5. (e) Instruction to each individual is comparable to the instruction that would be provided during a private lesson when the instruction involves more than one individual at a time; and

6. (f) The student-athlete does not use his or her name, picture or appearance to promote or advertise the avail- ability of fee-for-lesson sessions.

12.4.4 self-employment. [A] A student-athlete may establish his or her own business, provided the student-athlete's name, photograph, appearance or athletics reputation are not used to promote the business. (Ad- opted: 12/12/06, Revised: 8/7/14)

12.5.1.3 Continuation of Modeling and Other Non athletically Related Promotional Activities After Enrollment.[A] If an individual accepts remuneration for/or permits the use of his or her name or picture to advertise or promote the sale or use of a commercial product or service prior to enrollment in a member institution, continued remuneration for the use of the individual's name or picture (under the same or similar circumstances) after enrollment is permitted without jeopardizing his or her eligibility to participate in intercollegiate athletics only if all of the following conditions apply: (Revised: 1/14/97, 3/10/04, 8/7/14)

1. (a) The individual's involvement in this type of activity was initiated prior to his or her enrollment in a member institution;

2. (b) The individual became involved in such activities for reasons independent of athletics ability;

3. (c) No reference is made in these activities to the individual's name or involvement in intercollegiate athletics;

4. (d) The individual does not endorse the commercial product; and

5. (e) The individual's remuneration under such circumstances is at a rate commensurate with the individual's skills and experience as a model or performer and is not based in any way upon the individual's athletics ability or reputation.

Division II

Some rules are similar, while others may not be applied to Division II athletes.

12.4.1 Criteria Governing Compensation to Student-Athletes. Compensation may be paid to a student-athlete: (Revised: 11/22/04)

1. (a) Only for work actually performed; and

2. (b) At a rate commensurate with the going rate in that locality for similar services.

12.4.1.1 Athletics Reputation. Such compensation

may not include any remuneration for value or utility that the student-athlete may have for the employer because of the publicity, reputation, fame or personal following that he or she has obtained because of athletics ability.

12.4.2.2 Fee-for-Lesson Instruction. A student-athlete may receive compensation for teaching or coaching sports skills or techniques in his or her sport on a fee-for-lesson basis, provided all compensation received by the student-athlete is consistent with the criteria governing compensation to student-athletes (see Bylaw 12.4.1). (Adopted: 1/15/14)

12.5.1.2 Modeling and Other Non Athletically Related Promotional Activities. An individual may accept remuneration for or permit the use of his or her name or picture to advertise or promote the sale or use of a commercial product or service without jeopardizing his or her eligibility to participate in intercollegiate athletics only if all of the following conditions apply: (Revised: 1/14/97, 4/29/04, 1/8/07 effective 8/1/07)

(a) The individual became involved in such activities for reasons independent of athletics ability;

(b) No reference is made in these activities to the individual's involvement in intercollegiate athletics; (Revised: 1/18/14 effective 8/1/14)

(c) The individual's remuneration under such circumstances is at a rate commensurate with the individual's skills and experience as a model or performer and is not based in any way on the individual's athletics ability or reputation.

Division III

12.4.1 Criteria Governing Compensation to Student-Athletes. All compensation received by a student-athlete must be consistent with the limitations on financial aid set forth in Bylaw 15. Compensation may be paid to a student-athlete:

1. (a) Only for work actually performed; and
2. (b) At a rate commensurate with the going rate in that locality for similar services.

12.4.4 Fee-for-Lessons. A student-athlete may receive compensation for teaching or coaching sport skills or techniques in his or her sport on a fee-for-lesson basis, provided all compensation received by the student-athlete is consistent with the criteria governing compensation to student-athletes (see Bylaw 12.4.1). (Adopted: 7/31/12)

12.5.1.3 Modeling and Other Non Athletically Related Promotional Activities. It is permissible for an individual to accept remuneration for or permit the use of his or her name or picture to advertise or promote the sale or use of a commercial product or service without jeopardizing his or her eligibility to participate in intercollegiate athletics only if all of the following conditions apply: (Revised: 1/14/97, 1/12/04)

1. (a) The individual became involved in such activities for reasons independent of athletics ability;

2. (b) No reference is made in these activities to the individual's involvement in intercollegiate athletics; and

(Revised: 1/12/04)

3. (c) The individual's remuneration under such circumstances is at a rate commensurate with the individual's skills and experience as a model or performer and is not based in any way upon the individual's athletics ability or reputation.

Depending on which division you play in, there are more lax rules than others. If you are a NAIA athlete, there may be totally different requirements in order to start a business while playing collegiately. Theses rules may be confusing, but I have asked several compliance officers to help clear up any confusion and all the answers are similar to the questions that I have asked:

Q: Are student-athletes allowed to create their own businesses and sell their products while also competing collegiately?
A: Yes, they can, but they cannot use their likeness from being an athlete to promote their

businesses. Here is an example: A baseball player can start a computer programming business. However, he cannot advertise himself in the university uniform or that he plays college baseball.

Q: I know that NCAA rules prohibit the use of an enrolled student-athlete's name or picture to endorse a commercial product or service. What is considered a commercial product or service?
A: Anything which can be sold or revenue collected. For example: Our Health Services Department wanted to use our student-athletes in their uniforms for its flu shot advertisements. Even though Health Services is a university department, we could not allow it to happen because money is being made from the flu shots being purchased from the pharmaceutical supplier.

As far as possibly modeling for any company or product, then you would need to have that contract finalized before becoming a freshman or you would have to wait until your athletic career is over. Sorry for the bad news to all the aspiring models. I didn't make the rules. I am just the messenger, so please don't kill me. From the help of your coach and your compliance officer, you can successful start a business. There have been a few stories over the years of athletes either starting a t-shirt company, becoming a published author to running a book-borrowing company.

This story was actually in the early '90's. Greg Anthony was a basketball player at University of Nevada, Las Vegas (UNLV) while he and two of his friends created a business called "Two-Hype." It was a t-shirt and silk screening business where Anthony was making more than enough as a student-athlete entrepreneur to pay his own tuition. However, the NCAA declared that if he didn't give up his involvement in his business venture, he would be ineligible to play. Even though the NCAA ruled that having a business and paying one's way through school while playing a sport wasn't a conflict, some people thought it could allow boosters to channel their money through the business. In turn, that would cause a NCAA violation. Can you believe that? He was an athlete willing to commit his time, energy and possibly his own money to start a business and then had it shut down because of people's opinions. The former UNLV coach said, "These are three sharp kids who formed their own company, not something initiated by Boosters. It should be applauded."

In 2009, friends Erica Smith and Troy Rhodes Jr., launched a company called MyBookBorrow. Rhodes actually owned the company and Smith, who is a good friend of mine, acted as the chief operating office. She played basketball at a Division I university, so her books were paid for every semester. However, it this was not the case for most college students. The duo used "MyBookBorrrow" as a way to help make the college experience more affordable for students everywhere. The company offered textbook rentals to college students all over the country. She also used her network to help expand her company, while gaining valuable insight from successful business owners. During the start up phase, Rhodes and Smith had a lot of late nights and worked whenever they had a break. It took a lot of dedication and time management, but having additional people involved helped out a lot.

The company was nominated by Inc. Magazine as the "2010 Coolest College Start-ups." However, they ran into some challenges that were unforeseeable when launching. When you think about a textbook company of any kind, there are so many different textbooks on the market and creating a database to house all of those books was very difficult. At the time, they were not able to find anyone to build that database who did not want a lot of upfront money or to basically own a percentage of the company. Without an active online database, it was hard to compete with major players in the game. By 2010 college, bookstores were now in the market offering rentals as well. The two decided to part ways with the textbook industry and focus on other ventures.

Smith believes the experience she had starting a business was life changing. They had never run a business of that magnitude. But, it gave them a baseline to learn and grow for their next business opportunities. Smith is now a co-owner of a basketball academy in St. Louis, Mo. called Machine Elite Basketball Academy. She is also in the process of launching an organization called Second Wind. It will help prepare student-athletes to successfully transition out of college sports. She wants to teach student-athletes how to create and discover their own paths and to understand the role of entrepreneurship.

Smith believes student-athletes should have a plan and the courage to chase what they are destined for. It doesn't have to be a long extravagant business plan to start, but the goal is to know *what* you want to do, *why* you want to do it, *who* you are doing it for, and *how* are going to do it.

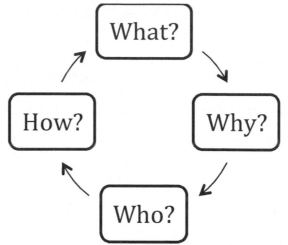

Get that figured out, seek out help and advice from your network and then go do it. Take that chance. Every experience we have in life only makes us better and helps us to grow if we let it. Launching a business as a student-athlete can be setting you up for amazing life.

What I am about to say may ruffle a few feathers. I am originally from a small town in Texas called Mexia. I tell people we have more cows than people. I earned a basketball scholarship to play at McClennan Community College, and then went to finish my playing career at Henderson State University in Arkadelphia, Ark. I recently finished my graduate degree at the University of Arkansas as well as worked in the athletic department with three of the women's teams. Usually, other teams in the Southeastern Conference (SEC) are not fond of each other because they are all competitors. However, I thought I would acknowledge Georgia football coach Mark Richt. I know what you are thinking, and no I am not a fan. I just love to give honor where it is due. Not only has he produced NFL players, but he has also supported some of his players to become filmmakers and authors while playing collegiately.

Chris Conley, who now plays in the NFL, created a 26-minute "Star Wars" fan film on the University of Georgia campus during his senior year in 2014. Because of the lack of knowledge that student-athletes have with the resources available to them, this project may have not been accomplished. Conley decided to ask for help and seek advice. With the help of the president, university, coach and players, the film was a success. There were tons of calls, meetings and sleepless night for Conley in order to complete his film.

"It's a good thing for people to hear that and see that — to realize that we're not just athletes, that we as football players aren't just good at football, that we can do other things as well," he said. "Pursue other dreams, but along with football. I don't think people realize we can do that."

During the summer of 2015, Georgia wide receive Malcolm Mitchell wrote a children's book called "The Magician's Hat." He used about $500 of his own money and self-published before starting his football season. He had to overcome NCAA rules for the promotion. He was not able to put a picture of himself in his football uniform on his website, and the university is unable to promote the book. However, they can promote his effort to encourage literacy. "I go through compliance every step of the way to make sure everything is going smooth," Mitchell said. "Our compliance office has done a great job of helping me. The NCAA has done an outstanding job of allowing me to do certain things." He actually used Conley's project to lay the foundation for launching his book.

Mitchell is now fulfilling his dream by playing in the NFL. As you read these stories about a few student-athletes who decided to create projects or business, I hope this gives you the motivation to help you on your own journey and gives you hope that this is indeed possible.

Both Conley and Mitchell created something that will soon create residual income if it has not already. Residual income is doing something one time and getting paid for it over and over again. For example, Michael Jackson wrote the song "Thriller" more than 30 years ago. Even though he has since passed away, his children will still profit for that song and others.

Before thinking about creating a business, make sure you ask the compliance director these questions to ensure you are following protocol:

- If asking for grants or sponsorships, would it be considered taking it as a gift according to the NCAA?

- Would it be extra benefits by providing my services or product to fans/donors?

CHAPTER 6

Business 101

"The way to get started is to quit talking and start doing." – Walt Disney

Before creating a business, you have to self-asses yourself. The answers to your questions below will help narrow your focus. This step is not supposed to dissuade you from starting your own business. Rather, it is here to get you thinking and planning. In order to start a successful business, passion alone is not enough. You need to plan, set goals and above all, know yourself.

Why do you want to start a business?

Is it the money, freedom, creativity or another reason?

What skills do you have?

What industries do you know about?

Would you want to provide a service or product?

What do you like to do?

Will it be full-time or part-time?

You can still work your business part-time while playing your sport. If you have graduated and now have a job, you can still do this part-time until you are making money to take care of yourself and your residual bills (those bills that come every first of the month whether you like it or not). Creating your business on the side creates options for people, and people LOVE OPTIONS!

With that being said, here are the six steps to starting your own business. I used these same steps as well when creating my second business. There are so many ways to effectively start your business that may be better than the steps I have provided. The key, regardless of what type of business you are starting, is to be flexible!

Develop An Idea

Every business that we know has started as an idea. Maybe you know of how you can fill the gap in a marketplace. Create a concept that you are passionate or knowledgeable about, and then turn that general idea into a specific idea. From there, come up with a product or service you believe that will enhance someone's life. A mentor of mine told me that a hobby is something that you like, but you should create a business that everyone wants. People do not buy what they need, the buy what they want.

Identify Your Market

In order to identify how attractive your prospective market really is, there are a few things you should consider:

How urgently do people need the thing you are selling or offering right now?

What's the market size? Are there already a lot of people paying for this product?

How easy is it (and how much will it cost you) to

acquire a customer?

How much money and effort will it cost to deliver the value you would like to be offering?

How long will it take to get to market? Will it take up to a month, a year or three years?

Will your business continue to be relevant as time passes? A business that repairs exclusively iPhone 5 screens will only remain relevant so long as the iPhone 5 sticks around. If your business is only relevant for a specific period of time, you will also want to consider your future plans.

If you like, you can even take things a step further and consider the consumer needs currently not being met by businesses in the industry. This is a good time to take a look at potential competitors. And remember, the presence of competitors is oftentimes a good sign! It means that the market for your product or service already exists. Therefore, you know that from the beginning, you are not flying entirely blind. While you have the time, learn as much as you can about your competitors, about what they provide to their customers, how they attract attention, and whether or not their customers are happy. If you can figure out what is missing before you even get started, your job will be made that much easier when you do finally create your business.

Take Advantage of Free Resources:

You are not only a collegiate athlete, but also a college student. There are many resources on campus, as well as the community to help you create a business. For example, the University of Arkansas has a center called the Small Business and Technology Development Center (ASBTDC). The ASBTDC is part of a national network of more than 1,000 small business development center offices that provide training, research and consulting services to existing and potential business owners. The Small Business and Technology Development Center (SBTDC) network is the largest small business assistance program in the United States. They offer free one-on-one consulting, seminars and research if your business is in the surrounding areas.

"Start Up Junkie Consulting" is community-based service for business owners as well. The United States Small Business Administration also funds them. "Startup Junkie Consulting" is a globally proven social venture. They help entrepreneurs build ventures at no cost to them, and help build venture communities around the world. They provide in-depth support, consulting and assistance to new ventures and small businesses from all industry verticals.

Currently, I am still using the services to help expand my business locally and globally. Even if your college or university does not have any services exactly like this, there are always other avenues and programs that are similar. Most colleges and universities have a business school and clubs for businesses. Join them or reach out to a professor in the department. I know they would be glad to help you in any way.

Business Plan

There are some entrepreneurs who never created a business plan to start their businesses and that is totally fine. But, depending on the need for investors, you may want to come up with a business plan. Each business plan is different. I was given a template that helped me figure out where my company was going, how it would overcome any potential difficulties and what I may need to sustain. Below are just a few things that should be included into your business plan:

- Executive summary (including business goals, objectives and desire amount if applying for a loan)
- Company Description (What does you company do?)
- Products and Services (The cost, features and benefits and/or cost of production)
- Marketing Strategy (How will you promote, distribute and/or sell? What customer service will you offer?)

- Financial Plans and Projections (The numbers that correspond to your written plan. Start-up cost expenses and capital)

You can also get a template from the Small Business Administration website at SBA.gov.

Select and Register Your Business Name

You can decide on a name that best fits you and your business. If you are planning to create several businesses under one umbrella, you can use your name as the business. For example, John Doe Enterprise. By using this process, the county and state now recognizes you as a real business. You also need to understand there are different legal entities before finalizing your business. Type of business entities included:

- Partnerships
- Sole proprietorship
- Corporation
- Limited Liability Company (LLC)

Spend some time knowing the pros and cons of each of the legal formation. Before starting my business, I attended a public seminar with the Sam Walton College Small Business Center titled "Choosing the Proper Legal Entity." The seminar was presented by Attorney Alex Miller of the law firm Reece, Moore and Pendergraft LLP. Reece, Moore and Pendergraft LLP assisted me at no charge in setting up my LLC and guiding me on how to operate my new legal entity. If at all possible, work with an attorney to iron out the details. This is not an area you want to get wrong. You will also need to get the proper business licenses and permits. Depending upon the business, there may be city, county or state regulations, and permits and licenses to deal with.

Continuous Improvement

There are more things you will need when you begin to create your business, as well as continuing on your entrepreneurial journey. Everyday, you should identify one to three actions that can further develop your business. Each small step is progress. As long as you are doing that, you will feel as if you are moving forward rather than staying in the same place.

Before even creating a business, I thought about starting a non-profit. I talked to several people and sought advice. I was told that it was quicker to start a business, and it was. I had all my paperwork and was in business in less than two weeks. Creating a non-profit is just as noble as creating a business. They both serve the same purpose and that is serving people. I am unable to tell you the exact steps to take in order to create a non-profit because I have not created one myself, but I know someone who has. I met Micah Dennis while I was working at the University of Arkansas. She is on the track team, competes in the shot put. She created the non-profit, "The Village: Easing Childhood Poverty." She launched her non-profit with a back-to-school event for children on August 6, 2016. The event was held on the University of Arkansas campus. The non-profit provided free food, free haircuts, free backpacks and schools supplies. There were also many Razorback athletes to meet.

She started "The Village: Easing Childhood Poverty" not only for personal reasons, but also for substantial social reasons. The organization gives children a home as well as a sense of social belonging and stability. Growing-up at times, she had neither. As a kid, she was okay with that; it was all she knew. Now that she is older, she understands the negative impact poverty can have on a child's life. Dennis understands how important it is to be the difference in a child's life. She wants to provide a safe space for children who might have a different environment at home.

The staff at the Office of Student-Athlete Success helped her establish her non-profit. "The staff was extremely helpful and encouraging," Dennis said. "They are so willing to listen and take the time to hear your story. I couldn't be more pleased with the staff. What I like most about our career development center is how they don't mind making changes, even if they've been doing something a certain way for years. They are for us, and all about us! If you are the person they believe you to be, you will be connected with the right people. In other words, allow the staff to truly know what it is you want and are striving for. Build relationships with the staff. They could become lifelong friends and business partners. And what I mean by 'right' is every connection is not a good connection; don't waste energy and time on people who are not for your benefit." Dennis only used compliance to learn what not to do.

I asked her how she was balancing her non-profit, classes and sports. She responded, "It is tough, yet satisfying. I find the balance of life exciting. I had to learn to put my social roles on a balance scale of positive to negative. School is a challenge in itself. I have trouble keeping up in school and always have. I love learning, but could not care less for the way we are taught in classrooms. I know I am going to have to lower my mood, feeling or frequency toward that role. Track is more of the positive role because of how much I am able to express myself and release any stress I may have. My coach and I have great communication and understanding of each other. It makes things go a lot smoother. "The Village E.C.P." is my passion. It is my all around happy place, my frequency vibrates the highest while in this role. I have no complaints. That is how I know what I am doing is supposed to happen. While running "The Village" bad things will and do happen, but I enjoy it just as much as the good things." Micah said the biggest thing she has learned so far is to listen to your intuition. Knowing yourself is your biggest strength. Regardless if you don't understand how to handle the situation, you are in a business debate — know what you are capable of.

Upon graduation, she will continue to run "The Village: E.C.P." She knows that it is her life's vision and what she went to school for. She even remembers making vision boards back in 2009. She could see what she wanted and it still looks the same. It's crazy how someone who is truly great knows before everyone else, but is left to make others see. There is no better way to show people how great you are than to step out of the only role they think you play and prove value in another way. Through her nonprofit, Dennis plans to give athletes jobs. Athletes are the super heroes of society to children and she sees how affective it is to connect the two.

Dennis' advice to current athletes who are pursuing entrepreneurship is "Go for it." Do not fear the greatness that comes with your hard work and the hard work that comes with greatness. As athletes, we get many incentives that regular students may not get. Use every resource possible while in school. It is free. In return, play the game, get everything you can out of the school. Network! This is the time to build relationships with your peers and find out what they want in life. You may find common interests and be able to team up.

CHAPTER 7

Faith > Fear

"If you are afraid of failure you don't deserve to be successful!" – Charles Barkley

Originally, this chapter was including in my book. Once I started writing more, I took the chapter out. The reason? I was fearful, and wanted to stay in my comfort zone. There is an old saying, "Everything you have every wanted is on the other side of your comfort zone." Everyone deals with fears and I am not excluded; I just felt it did not need to be addressed. But whenever you feel scared about promoting a business, company, program, experience you are a part of, think of those who will be affected by you not sharing your story. With that being said, let's talk about faith over fear.

I fear failing. Yes, I said it. I fear failing my parents, my siblings, my grandparents and my entire family. I fear failing those who believe in me, and most of all, I fear failing myself. We all have high hopes and dreams of making our friends, family and significant others proud. But, the fear of failing still lingers in the back of our minds.

Because of my personality, I do not tell a lot of people my dreams and my subsequent moves. If people do not know your dreams, then they cannot shoot them down. I learned the hard way. One day, I met with someone I highly respected for brunch. I remember I was so excited because it had been a while since we last spoke. We were enjoying our meal, and then he asked me the big question, "What do you plan on doing upon gradation?" That question would always make me very uncomfortable. Not because I did not know what I wanted to do with my life after graduation, but because I was very protective of my dreams. I then said, "I don't know yet." He goes on to say "Krystal, you are graduating in less than a month and you have no idea what you are going to do?" In my head, I'm saying to myself, "I already know what I am going to do, but I am just not telling you." I then say, "Well, I know what I am going to do and I have been knowing for the last couple of months."

I begin to tell him my plans for the next five years and the projects I was working on. As soon as I am finished, he has the nerve to say, "Well, you don't look like a business woman to me." I just began to look at him and ponder, "How does a business woman look -- or even a business man?" My father, works 40-60 hours a week with oil mechanic clothes on, operates a six-figure automotive shop on an 8th grade education. So what does a businessman or woman technically look like? After that sentence, I did not really remember anything else about our conversation. Initially, I wasn't bothered by the comment, but subconsciously, it brought a kind of fear in my mind. Fear of what if I could not execute the plans I had, the fear of not leading a team, the fear of not fulfilling my own self-prophecy. I then remembered one of my mentors telling me, "If you buy a person's opinion, then you buy their lifestyle." I am not saying he did not have a great lifestyle, but I knew he was capable of something more and was settling. So again, you can not let other people's opinion scare you into not chasing your dreams, not creating something you have always dreamed of, or not living in your purpose. Do not ever let someone talk you out of your dreams. If anyone ever tells you your dreams are silly, remember there is a millionaire walking around who invented the pool noodle!

Growing up, I felt like public speaking was going to be the death of me. I was the shy kid in school and used to dread presentations in class. If we had group projects, I wanted to be in charge of doing the presentation and would let everyone else present. I was that girl. Once in high school, the teachers started making everyone do presentation by themselves. In my head, I was panicking. I would think of all the ways I could get out of it. Can I become ill? No, because it was a game day. Maybe

I could just skip that class. Nope, can not do that because the teacher is cool with all the coaches. You all just do not understand how I was feeling. The Huffington Post says that public speaking is one of America's top fears, along with heights and bugs. Now, I feel a little better because there are millions of people who feel the same way as me.

On the day of my presentation, my PowerPoint was looking nice with all the creative templates, transitions and animations. I stared into the crowd and saw my friends making silly faces at me, my high school crush on his phone, one of my classmates picking her nose and the rest of the class waiting on me to start. To be honest, I do not even remember what I said. I naturally talk fast. My grandfather tells me I must be Hispanic because I talk fast and he can never understand me. I always tell him, "I'm not talking fast, you are just listening slow, like Lil' Wayne says."

During my presentation, I am talking 10 times my normal speed, hands are shaking like I have paralysis and I feel like I am sweating profusely.

Once I was finished, everyone began clapping for me. I was sure it was out of pity. I felt awful and when I went back to my seat, I had an underarm sweat circle. Over the next few years, most of my presentation were like that. But guess what? My speeches and presentation began to progress. The underarm sweat circle started to decrease in size. Today, my hands no longer shake uncontrollably, but they do still tremble from time to time. I am now able to slow my speech down, even though I sometimes still speak fast if I get excited or anxious. The lesson here is if you do what you fear the most, and the death of fear is certain.

Starting a business can be scary. You are selling yourself and/or your product. When I was younger, I had to do different fundraisers for band, sports or Girl Scouts. Yes, I was something like a band geek. Let's not judge. My parents put my siblings in anything that could possibly help us earn a scholarship. I was so shy that I would ask my mom to take my Girl Scout cookie order form to her job and ask her colleagues. I would then get irritated if she did not sell anything. When I first started my business, it was so weird sharing my product with people, and then asking them to buy it. I felt like I was not cut out to be the successful entrepreneur because I couldn't sell a thing. After nearly two years, I realized that we all have the potential to be to make a sale. Whether it is the student-athletes selling themselves (athletic talent) to possibly get a scholarship; or the coach selling the athlete the dream of the impact they could make once becoming part of the team; or the famous singers and actors. We are all selling something. As long as you have the haves, you'll always have the have nots.

Remember in the introduction I mentioned about writing my book in 2020 because I knew I would be more successful? While that is true, I was really fearful of writing it. I wasn't sure if my story was compelling enough. I was afraid of my book not selling, or the people of NCAA institutions debunking the facts or the student-athletes ability to create a business while also competing collegiately.

Fear can cripple us from achieving some of our wildest dreams. Fear is only an illusion of things that have not even happened yet. Even though these are my fears, I decide to do it anyway. Over the last four years, I have implemented a few exercises that have helped activate my faith and conquer some of my biggest fears.

Re-Wire the Brain

- Affirmations - They are really simple. They are you being in conscious control of your thoughts. They are short and powerful statements. When you say them, think of them, or even hear them, they become thoughts that create your reality. Affirmations make you consciously aware of your thoughts. I have affirmations around my mirror and my room that help me re-wire my brain. My top five that I make sure to tell myself everyday are:

- I am grateful for all people and all things in my life. They are all purposeful to my growth and happiness.
- I choose to open myself to new connections and opportunities everyday.
- My products and services are unique and innovative. They are popular and attractive to international clients and partners.
- I have a gifted passion, courage, commitment and integrity for my happiness and success.
- I believe I can be whatever I want to be.

There are hundred of affirmations that you can say to help you overcome your fears. There are even some affirmations that can be used for being an athlete. You just have to find the right affirmations that fit you and the vision for your life. They are simple tasks that will change your life.

- Books - I only read personal development and financial books. I have grown more as a person within the last four years. I wish I would have implemented this process earlier in my teen years. I take at least 30 minutes before I go to sleep or when I wake up to read 10 pages a day.

- Audios - Listen to 20 minutes of motivational speaking, podcasts that talk about becoming successful or what it takes to get there. That also helps you conquer your fears because you are hearing someone else tell their story. You can even add in some inspirational music that will help you get through the day.

Do ONE thing every day that scares you

I have already told you about my fears with writing this book. There were some days I made myself write at least 500 words. I knew writing would allow me to finish my book, but also help me because in spite of the fear I had, I was doing it. So if it is that sell you need to make, do it anyway. If you are afraid to ask for help because someone may so no, do it anyway. If you are scared to ask someone to be your mentor, ask anyway. Once you start doing things despite your fear, you will start having a sense of accomplishment and a feeling of "that wasn't so bad." As I am telling you this, I am still learning to do this myself.

I realized a long time ago that the cemetery is the richest place in the world. I have seen too many people go to their graves with their dreams still in them. Settling for a life of less. Songs never sung, books never written, works never completed, businesses never started, levels of success and personal fulfillment never achieved. Do not be another dash of unfulfilled promise resting eternally on a pile of excuses buried underneath fear, poverty, consciousness, limited belief and your crappy story as to why you cannot, will not or do not deserve a greater life with greater results! Change can happen in an instant. The work required to maintain it can be a lifetime and it will all be worth it! Decide to take a chance on you and your dreams —

they will soon become reality.

CHAPTER 8

The A.R.C. Effect

"The quality of a person's life is in direct proportion to their commitment to excellence, regardless of their chosen field of endeavor." – Vince Lombardi

The A.R.C. is actually an acronym that means Action Reveals Commitment. Since you are reading this book, that shows that I was committed to finishing this book. You probably have a few ideas in your life that you have started building and never finished, right? Whether you are looking to change the world or, at the very least, help change the lives of a few people, I want to kick this chapter off with an activity. I want you to pull out your pen and list off the last three things you started and never completed.

Here is my list:

1. Finishing my teacher certification;
2. Knee rehabilitation after 2nd surgery;
3. Creating a non-profit to help children;

Now...

Your list:

1. _____

2. _____

3. _____

Congratulations on taking the time to be honest with yourself about your incomplete projects and unfinished ideas! Facing our failures can be tough. Do not look at this list and feel defeated. The journey you are currently on and succeeding at is proof that determination can take you far. This activity is just an eye-opener for you, but can you be committed to go back and complete one of those things on your list?

What "Off-Season?"

I keep saying that being a collegiate athlete and entrepreneurship go hand-in-hand. Being a student-athlete is a full time job, plus overtime, and the job never ends. We have pre-season, in-season and then off-season. Let's not even talk about the summer commitment. Summer is not the time off for college athletes. You should expect to be putting in 10 to 15 hours per week minimum during the summer to prepare yourself for the upcoming athletic season. I even complied a chart to help put it in perspective of the life of a student-athlete. This chart does not include classes/labs, homework, study groups or social hours.

- Practice
- Coach initiated meetings
- Game film review
- Required camps or clinics
- Required weight training or conditioning
- Compliance meeting
- Traveling to/from competition site
- Recruiting activities (ex: student host)
- Training room activities

- Fundraising activities and community service projects

When I first got offered an athletic scholarship, I was on an emotional high. It was like puppy love. It was all fun and games until some of my close teammates started getting cut. I remember there were many times that I wanted to give up and be a regular student who did not have to worry about the coaches, practices and long days. I stepped out of my emotions and stepped into commitment. There were days when I hated going to practice, game film sessions or weights. But I was committed to become the best student-athlete I could be. I was committed to being the best player on my team and helping my team win. Imagine if you could take that same mindset and apply it to creating something while playing collegiality.

I have talked with several athletes about the time commitment obstacle that we have all faced while playing sports in college. You may be going through this same process right now. But do you remember the saying, "You make time for what you want." That is so true on so many levels. I get it. Student-athletes do not have a lot of time, but imagine if you could stop watching television for an hour and work on a business plan? What if you stayed up an extra hour researching people you should connect with to get your business going? Time management is about perspective. What are some things that are not helping you grow that can be taken away?

Once I started my business as a student-athlete, I sold my television. That was one of the hardest decision of my life. I was addicted to the reality, criminal and law shows. And, of course, Sports Center and the Top 10 Plays segment. I knew that was a distraction that would not allow me to be committed to my business. I am not much of a party girl, but I would sometimes go with my teammates and socialize. I began to limit those social engagements to spend time learning and working my business. There were times I would miss all the drama, or hear my teammates talk about all the fun they had while they were celebrating. But I knew the actions I was taking revealed the commitment I made to myself and my business. Imagine if you were to use seven hours out of your week to dedicate to create a business:

7 (Hours)

X 4 (Weeks in a month)

28 hours for one month

28 (hours per month)

X 12 (months in a year)

336 hours for one year

These numbers are just a sample of putting time in perspective. I would hope you are able to put more hours into creating something in your "off season" or during the summer. Time is your only asset, and it is the only thing you cannot get back.

The 409 Story

Every Saturday was cleaning day for my family and me. Actually it was more like my siblings and me with my mom. My dad was either working hard at his business or refereeing to make some extra cash. I was usually in charge of cleaning the kitchen or the bathroom. I loved using Formula 409 because it made cleaning all those greasy stains even easier. I would spray the product on the stains and leave it on for two to five minutes. Afterward, it would wipe off so clean; there was never a need for old fashion elbow grease — as my grandmother would say. Only a couple months ago, I knew the story behind the product and was totally shocked. There were two young scientists that committed to creating the greatest all-purpose cleaner this world had ever seen. The ultimate cleaner did not happen on the first try. It did not even happen on the 150th or the 308th try. It was not until the 409th try that scientists were able to discover the perfect chemical mixture to formulate the grease cutting, dirt destroying, bacteria cutting cleaner. Can you imagine being committed to a project, a skill or a business until you are satisfied with the outcome?

Oftentimes, we let our emotions get the best of us when things are not going as planned. There needs to be a time when you step out of emotions and step into commitment. This world today does not demand that of people. The world wants us to go through the motions, but never demands commitment. It is okay to be average as long as you try. That is not the case when you become a student-athlete or an entrepreneur. Action is the only way to reveal commitment, not only to your sport, but also to your project and/or business.

CHAPTER 9

Root Beer Budget, Champagne Dreams

"Don't tell me where your priorities are. Show me where you spend your money and I'll tell you what they are." —James W. Frick

Starting any business has a price; you will need to determine how you are going to cover the costs. Depending on the type of business you are trying to create, the start up cost can be very low. I have met tons of entrepreneurs who have started a business for $50-$1,000 of their own money.

Here are a few examples:

- Become a professional photographer. If you have a passion for photography, creating family portraits or taking photos at events for people, photography could be the start of a profitable business. It is complex because you will need a nice camera. If you can get a great deal on a good camera or already have one, then the start-up costs are low.

- Start a tutoring business where you can teach another language, musical instrument, computer, cooking, chemistry or whatever you have to offer.

- Be a consultant. Every industry could use a consultant. Just make sure you have success in that particular field.

- Write a book. Turn your passion into a mission to educate others and self-publish it. Create a good story. Find your target audience. Find a great editor and self-publish.

- Become a representative for a direct sales company. You do not have to worry about creating a product or inventing a business structure. If you like talking to people, this social business could be for you. Incomes differ based on the company you work for and the amount of sales you make.

- Become a social media influencer. As I have mentioned before, student-athletes already have a platform. You can create your own brand through social media. Target a niche and keep your content focused around the particular them

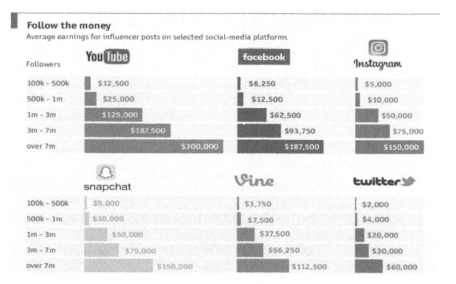

Follow the money

Average earnings for influencer posts on selected social-media platforms

Followers	YouTube	facebook	Instagram
100k - 500k	$12,500	$6,250	$5,000
500k - 1m	$25,000	$12,500	$10,000
1m - 3m	$125,000	$62,500	$50,000
3m - 7m	$187,500	$93,750	$75,000
over 7m	$300,000	$187,500	$150,000

	snapchat	Vine	twitter
100k - 500k	$5,000	$3,750	$2,000
500k - 1m	$10,000	$7,500	$4,000
1m - 3m	$50,000	$37,500	$20,000
3m - 7m	$75,000	$56,250	$30,000
over 7m	$150,000	$112,500	$60,000

- Graphic Designer. There are free design tools out there for everyone, but many do not offer customized designs. That can be very frustrating for the non-designer. This is the perfect time for when your business could come in and save the day.

- Personal Fashion Stylist. You can start with your friends and encourage them to share with others. Soon, you could have or own profitable fashion business.

- Personal Trainer. Athletes are made to work out to stay in shape and prepared for the season. If you absolutely have a passion for working out, then becoming a personal trainer can be for you. Put your money toward your certifications, books, workshops, conferences, mentorships, and internships. Your social media should have you attracting potential clients, posting about nutrition and you working out in the gym.

- Moving company or professional landscaping business. This can be a perfect business if you are staying in the area during the summer. You could buy lawn mowing equipment. You could even give your cards out to people asking for referrals. Also, around this time, many people are moving out or it may be too hot. People in the community could hire you to help them move or even mow their lawn. You could even make it more affordable.

While many entrepreneurs put their own money into their new companies, it's very possible that you'll need financial assistance. A commercial loan through a bank is a good starting point, although these are often difficult to secure. If you are unable to take out a bank loan, you can apply for a small business loan through the Small Business Administration (SBA).

Bootstrapping

When I started my first business, I did not have a lot of money, but I began with what I had. You will most likely have to do the same. Any money that I received, earned or worked for would go back into my business. I would not go buy new clothes, new shoes or the "next best electronic device." I remember vividly when my teammates would go buy the newest Jordan's, huge 50-inch flat screens or spend money on new outfits or liquor for the nightclubs. Instead, I spent it on personal development seminars and ways to grow my business. I was frugal while in college. Of course, I made sure I got the clothes I needed rather than wanted. I spent money on the necessities and invested the rest of my money into my business. There was this personal development seminar that I really wanted to attend. I had already paid for my plane ticket and the cost needed for the event, but I wanted extra money for food, activities or anything miscellaneous. I rummaged through my things looking for something to sell. I was lying down on my bed after one of my basketball games. It popped in my head. All I do anyways in my free time is watch ESPN, Criminal Minds, and Law & Order: SVU. I decided to put my television up for sale. I had a DVD player and I knew I would not need that either since I would no longer have a TV, so I sold that, too. Sometimes the distractions can cost you money, but in my case, it made me money when I sold it. People think when you first start a business, you need a half a million dollars to just get your business off the ground. Within the new era, it is certainly easier now than ever before.

CHAPTER 10

Failing Forward

I've missed more than 9,000 shots in my career. I've lost almost 300 games; 26 times, I've been trusted to take the game winning shot and missed. I've failed over and over and over again in my life. And that is why I succeed. — Michael Jordan

When you decided to read this book, you decided to join me on the journey of becoming a student-athlete entrepreneur. Together we have explored a new way of thinking and how we can use our skills and resources to become entrepreneurs. These are the strategies to help you win! I hope this book has given you the tools to guide your career. From deciding what you want to do, when and why to make a change in your career, and whether you would like pursuing the entrepreneur journey full-time or part-time. I bet you have heard the old saying, "Life is a marathon, not a sprint." The same applies to becoming an entrepreneur. When you first began playing your sport at a young age, you were not in the same position to go play at a college or university. It took years to perfect your craft. Take the same time, commitment and determination and apply it now.

According to the Small Business Administration 2016 statistics, nearly half of all employer establishments survive at least five years and a third survive 10 years or more. Almost 80 percent survived more than one year. While according to Forbes, eight out of 10 entrepreneurs who start businesses fail within the first 18 months. That is really a startling number if you think about it. However, you cannot let the fear of failing enter your mind. Most businesses do not fail due to their product or services, but most their lack of marketing. There are three ways to promote your business without even using social media.

Personal Communication Marketing - You can achieve this with calling potential clients or sending emails.

Personal Touch Marketing – This can happen when you physically shake someone's hand at a networking event or some other type of function and you either exchange contact information for a follow-up or give them your business card.

Force Visibility Marketing – This happens when the first two haven't worked or you haven't received any traction. I recently did this with my current start up. I went to a local high school football game and put flyers on cars until I no longer had any flyers. I printed more than 500 copies. The fans, parents and players were forced to see something on their windshields once they got into their vehicles after the game.

You could pay for marketing, which is so much

easier than doing it yourself, or you can learn as you go — especially if you are short on cash.

Here are some marketing strategies to do for free or at a low cost to you and your business:

Create a website so your customers and potential clients will get a better understanding of you, what you do and how you can add value to their lives.

Network at your local Chamber of Commerce. This is a classic marketing idea for small businesses because it can bring in revenue. Association with the Chamber will make your events more credible, and you can find new partners or clients, or discover opportunities to teach or speak.

Speak at seminars and teach workshops. You will get publicity from marketing the event from the event itself. Besides, you will look more professional in your customers' eyes.

Send handwritten holiday, birthday or thank you cards to past or current clients, valued partners, vendors in your referral network, or contacts who have helped you. You can buy a variety of thank you cards at the Dollar Tree or Dollar Store for the price of a $5 box from Popeye's. This is a low-cost and unique marketing idea for a small business.

Host FREE events. Reporters are always looking for a good story. Give them what they want and get some free publicity by hosting a free event. You will get more of a response if there is food or freebies involved.

Offer FREE consultation. Free consultations are a great way to showcase your expertise and get more clients.

Imprint company logo on hats and T-shirts. Your loyal customers will be happy to wear them, and will become free brand promoters.

Exceed your customer expectations. Reputation is everything these days. By exceeding your customer expectations and walking the extra mile, you will drive more business.

Ask your customers for referrals. Beat your shyness. Simply ask — and you will receive.

Create value. Invest your time and energy in building a great product that creates value for your customers. If you manage to do that, the product is selling itself.

I recently read a story about Kevin Hart and his journey of what one may say was an "overnight success." For more than 15 years, Hollywood executives told Kevin Hart that he was not good enough or funny enough. Hollywood executive told him that he lacked the "IT" factor to become a star and to take a hike. During those years, Hart never sulked, never felt sorry for himself or made excuses.

He worked and worked. He worked on personal development, improving his skills, increasing his knowledge, understanding the industry and perfecting his craft. After more than 15 years, he became an overnight success. In the last 12 months, Hart surpassed Jerry Seinfeld to become the highest paid comedian in the world — with earnings of $87.5 million. Imagine if you could dedicate the next 10-15 years to your passion and get good at something worth getting good at.

The most important thing you can do now is to start spending time with people who are entrepreneurs or who have relationships with people in that industry. There are a lot of people that glamourize that side of entrepreneurship. Let me tell you from experience, it is extremely hard. You will want to quit and you will be broke. People will think you are crazy, but if you can make it through all of this, you will make it.

To begin your entrepreneurial journey, you first need to find a mentor. I have several mentors who serve different purposes in my life, but all challenge me and expect me to progress. Some of my mentors do not even know they are mentors to me. For example, David Shands, the man I mentioned in Chapter 3. He created "Sleepis4suckers" and also wrote the book called "Dreams Are Built Overnight." I also watch all of his YouTube videos. Successful people can be your mentors without ever meeting them. If you can find a mentor who you meet with on a weekly or monthly basis, then that would be perfect. Right now, I have five mentors who help me stay on track to becoming successful who I could call or meet with. Being able to have a mentor can alleviate a lot of those things you will go through, as well as help you with ways on how to prevent some struggles.

As athletes, we always have a schedule. Most of the time, our coach and professors make our schedules. Once your eligibility is up or you graduate, you will realize all the time you have. The easiest thing to start doing is create a strict schedule that will keep you on track with creating your business and working on your business. Since you will start working for yourself, then you will not have a boss. Your schedule is now your boss. Since graduating, I am still struggling with making my own schedule and sticking to it. Sometimes, we can get so sidetracked with other things or people that we forget to focus. I make a to-do list right before I go to bed so once I wake up, I know what needs to be done. I also block out times for each task so I can only focus on task at a time instead of multitasking. Most times, we do not get much done with multitasking. Or maybe, it's just me.

You should learn and study from other people. If you are creating a blog and struggling with getting subscribers, reach out to a fellow blogger. Most are willing to help and offer advice. Thankfully, I have been able to come in contact with some people who have been willing to either help me or grow with them while I have been on my entrepreneurial journey; it has certainly been a blessing. I know everyone is not meant to become an entrepreneur and I am definitely content with that. However, I do think it is important to be a dream chaser and a goal getter. Your dreams stretch and push you to unimaginable heights and pull things out that you did not know were there. They haunt you at night and bring mornings to your doorstep before you have slept a wink. Goal setting and goal getting are the keys to unlocking the realization of your dreams. Goals empower you to measure your activity, effort and progress. They are the steps to greater success. You should be chasing after a dream with as much vigor as you do a woman or a man, a seat at the salon, entry into the night club, tickets to the sporting event or the pair of the latest designer shoes. If you are not setting and getting daily goals that will move you closer to living out your dreams, then you are missing out on life's greatest gifts and the opportunity to realize the person you thought you could never become.

Life is about chances. Playing sports is about chances. Going pro after college is about chances.

A few weeks ago, I was listening to Sports Center and heard the interview Stephen A. Smith and Tim Tebow had about Tebow deciding to pursue baseball over pro football. He said something that really resonated with me and I felt was appropriate for the book.

Tebow said, "When are dreams based on chances? Dreams are based on something that is in your heart. They are passions based on something that you want to try, not chances." He went on to critique the complacency we have in our society.

"What's unfortunate in society is that a lot of people just do what they feel like they should do, and live by all these rules... just go and accept your average [9-to-5 job] rather than striving for something. Because the ultimate goal isn't to succeed or fail. The ultimate goal is to give it everything you have for something in your heart and a dream and pursing that. And if you get to live out your dream every single day, then the result doesn't matter. I can look back 20, 30 years from now and be able to look at this time and say, "You know what? I gave everything I had to football. I gave everything I had to baseball. And I was able to live out some dreams. In my opinion, that's pretty awesome."

Notes

Estimated probability of competing in professional athletics.

http://www.ncaa.org/about/resources/research/estimated-probability-competing-professional-athletics

2016-2017 NCAA Division I manual.

https://www.ncaapublications.com/p-4435-2016-2017-ncaa-division-i-manual-august-version-available-august-2016.aspx

2016-2017 NCAA Division II manual.

http://www.ncaapublications.com/p-4436-2016-2017-ncaa-division-ii-manual-august-version-available-august-2016.aspx

2016-2017 NCAA Division II manual.

https://www.ncaapublications.com/p-4390-2015-2016-ncaa-division-iii-manual-august-version-available-august-2015.aspx

Acknowledgements

"Wow.. I just don't know what to say... This is SO unexpected... First, I'd like to thank the Academy..."

I've always wanted to win me an Academy Award and I know I would have a lot of people to thank and I would tell a story about why I was thanking each one, but I will keep it short for the sake of time. I would like to thank God who has allowed me to use the gifts and talents given to me to inspire others to achieve their dreams! As strange as it may sound, I would also like to thank myself for not allowing others to taint my dreams. I know that may seem odd to you, but I have always given so much of myself to others and has hardly ever accepted the honor. So today, I will accept the honor, but I will not take the glory that belongs to my Father in Heaven! So speaking internally, "Krystal, you are truly an inspiration to me. Thank you."

Thank you to my parents, Kelvin and Culetta Beachum for raising this special child of yours. In your words, I am so special that I don't even know how special I am. To my siblings, Kelvin, Jacob and Brechelle, thank you for your contributions to my life as your sister and as a social entrepreneur. To my grandparents, J.W. & Lurlean Beachum and O'Dell and Betty Harris, I am truly the product of your prayers.

A special thank you to the organizations and people that have molded my life and my thoughts throughout my student-athlete journey and those who are still helping me along the way: Mexia High School, McLennan Community College, Henderson State University, University of Arkansas, Cameron Chapel, Tate Temple, Salvation Lighthouse, Patricia Harris, Coach Arthur Pertile, Coach Dobie Smith, Coach Ricky Rhodes, Coach Randy Barger, Coach Leven Barker, Coach Kyle Wilson, Coach Anthony Branch, Coach Jill Thomas, Coach Kaci Bailey, Dr. Kenneth Taylor, Dr. Ceyla Taylor, Martha Londagin, Jay Amargos, Tim Lampkin, Kale Gober, Anaas Hobbs, Angela Lewis, Erica Smith, Micah Dennis, Mike Hairston, and the rest of my family and friends. Your impact will reach way beyond our lifetime.

About the Author

Krystal grew up in a small town called Mexia, Texas. It was there that she learned her greatest values in being successful, which are respect, discipline and hard work! As she grew into her own person, she found great support from her family, teachers and teammates, which ignited her passion for athleticism and creating her personal brand.

Krystal has been blessed to graduate with her Associates degree from McLennan Community College, acquired her Bachelor's degree from Henderson State University where she broke the Conference and school record by scoring 41 points in a single game, and went on to achieve her Master's degree in Education in Recreation and Sports Management through University of Arkansas.

In May of 2016, Krystal founded Student-Athletes Unite where the mission is to educate high school athletes on recruiting, inspiring current athletes to become entrepreneurs, and connect student athletes domestically and internationally.

Krystal currently lives in Fayetteville, Arkansas and spends her time traveling the world, inspiring others through public speaking engagements and one-on-one consulting.